# Daniel
## Asks About
# Baptism and Communion

*May God
Never forget
Jesus loves*

*bless you!
how much
you!*

*Love,*

*Heather Hanna* x

# Heather J. Hanna

**Pacific Press® Publishing Association**
Nampa, Idaho
Oshawa, Ontario, Canada
www.pacificpress.com

Book design by Dennis Ferree
Cover and inside illustrations by Marcus Mashburn

ISBN: 0-8163-2083-7
Library of Congress Cataloging-in-Publication Data

Hanna, Heather.
Daniel asks about baptism and Communion/Heather Hanna.
p. cm.
ISBN 0-8163-2083-7
1. Baptism—Seventh-Day Adventists—Juvenile literature. 2. Lord's Supper—
Seventh-Day Adventists—Juvenile literature. 3. Seventh-Day Adventists—
Doctrines—Juvenile literature.
I. Title.

BX6154.H298 2005
264'.06732081—dc22                                    2005043129

Additional copies of this book are available by calling
toll free 1-800-765-6955 or by visiting
http://www.AdventistBookCenter.com

05 06 07 08 09 · 5 4 3 2 1

## Dedication
To Daniel, Michael, and Lez with all my love.
To Barbara and Ivor Margerison and Bob and Rae
Hanna, our parents, who told us the stories that we
now pass on to our children and taught us to love
God with all our hearts.
To all my friends who inspire me—may God hold
you in the palm of His hand.

# 1

# Daniel
## Asks About
# Baptism

**D**aniel was excited about a very special Sabbath. He lay in bed thinking about it. Aunt Angie and Uncle John were going to be baptized at church that day.

Daniel knew that Mommy and Daddy were excited as well. They had often prayed for Aunt Angie and Uncle John. They wanted Aunt Angie and Uncle John to know and love Jesus.

**D**aniel got up and went to find Mommy.

"What will happen at church today?" Daniel asked on Sabbath morning.

"Well," Mommy said, "Pastor David will ask Aunt Angie and Uncle John to stand up front in church. He will ask them whether they love Jesus and want to follow Him. They will say 'Yes.' Then they will go out. They will get changed into special clothes that can get wet.

"At the front of the church there is a big tank of water. Aunt Angie and Uncle John and Pastor David will walk down into the tank. The water comes up only to their middle. Pastor David will dip them under the water for just a second."

"Why do they do that?" Daniel asked.

Mommy smiled. "Aunt Angie and Uncle John will show everyone that they want their old, sinful life to go away, and they want to live a happy new life with Jesus."

**W**hat happens next?" Daniel wanted to know.

"They walk up out of the water tank and go and dry off," Mommy said. "They come back to the front of the church. Everyone in the church welcomes them into their new life with Jesus."

**W**ill they be scared when they go under the water?"
Daniel wondered.

"No. It is just for a moment," Mommy replied. "Are you scared
when you are under the water when you go swimming?"

"No," Daniel said.

"Aunt Angie and Uncle John won't be scared at all," Mommy
said. "They will be very happy. Now let's get dressed in our
Sabbath clothes. We don't want to be late!"

**A**nd sure enough, it all happened at church just as Mommy had said. Daniel watched as Pastor David and Aunt Angie and Uncle John stepped into the water tank. Pastor David raised his hand and spoke. Then he dipped Aunt Angie quickly under the water and then lifted her up. Then he did the same with Uncle John.

**E**veryone was very happy, especially Laura, Aunt Angie and Uncle John's daughter. Daniel gave Laura a gift to help her remember the special day. He gave her a children's picture Bible.

At bedtime that evening after Sabbath was over, Mommy sat on Daniel's bed.

"Did you have a nice day?" Mommy asked.

"Oh, yes," Daniel said. "What is my story about tonight?"

**D**aniel's story was about Jesus. Mommy told him that Jesus was baptized by His cousin, John the Baptist. A light from God shone down from heaven. God said, "This is my beloved Son, and I am very pleased with Him." Then the Holy Spirit came down to Jesus in the form of a dove.

"Wow, that must have been a very special baptism," Daniel said.

"Yes. All baptisms are special," Mommy said. "The Bible says everyone in heaven is very happy when someone chooses to follow Jesus.

"Now let's pray."

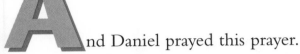nd Daniel prayed this prayer.

"Dear God,

"Thank You for Aunt Angie and Uncle John and Laura. Thank You that they decided to follow You. Thank You for Mommy and Daddy and the baby we are going to have. Thank You for loving us. And please look after us all. In Jesus' name, amen."

"When I grow up, can I be baptized, Mommy?" Daniel asked. "I want to follow Jesus too."

"Of course, darling. I'll be very proud of you when you do," Mommy said. She leaned down to kiss Daniel goodnight. Daniel snuggled down to sleep.

THE END

# 2

# Daniel
## Asks About
# Communion

**D**aniel couldn't wait to get to church. Mommy had told him that the service was a very special one. They would think about how Jesus saves us from our sins.

# W

hat does it mean, Mommy, that 'Jesus saves us from our sins'?" Daniel asked.

"Well," Mommy said, "when we do something wrong, God calls it a sin. Our sins make Jesus sad. When Jesus died a long time ago, He took the blame for our sins so that we wouldn't have to."

"Oh-h-h-h-h," Daniel said, "that was very nice of Jesus."

"Yes," Mommy said. "Then Jesus came back to life and went up to His home in heaven. Now, all we have to do is believe that Jesus loves us and will take the blame, no matter what we have done, and we will live with Him forever in heaven.

"Now let's hurry and get ready for church!"

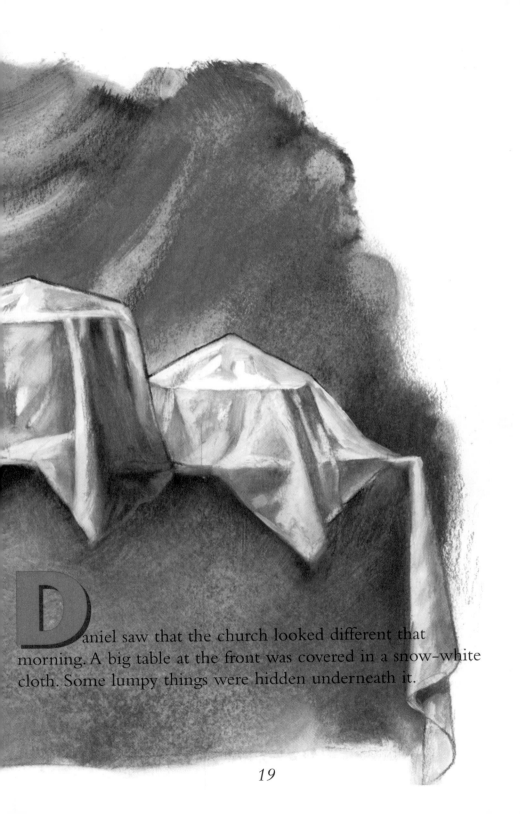

Daniel saw that the church looked different that morning. A big table at the front was covered in a snow-white cloth. Some lumpy things were hidden underneath it.

**S**oon it was time for the children's story. Daniel ran to the front of the church. He sat down next to the other boys and girls.

Miss Velda told the story of the last Last Supper. That was the meal Jesus ate with His disciples before He died. She said that Jesus told us to eat bread and drink juice at church sometimes.

It helps us to remember how very much Jesus loves us. Miss Velda called it Communion. Then she sent the children back to their seats.

**D**aniel watched as people got up to leave. Some women went into one room. Some men went into another. Mommy and Daddy walked to a room with lots of mommies and daddies, and Daniel followed.

He saw Daddy praying with Mommy. Then Daddy fetched a bowl of water. He set it down in front of Mommy. She took off her shoes. Daddy knelt in front of Mommy and poured the water over her feet. Then he dried her feet with a towel.

"What does the water feel like?" Daniel asked.

"It's warm," Mommy said with a smile. She pulled her shoes back on.

Mommy took the bowl of water to a table. Then she brought back another bowl of water. Daddy took off his socks and shoes.

Daniel asked, "What are you doing this for?"

**D**addy told him, "Washing feet is called the ordinance of humility. Jesus washed the feet of His disciples. Do you remember that story? Washing feet was the job of a servant. The disciples did not want to do it. But Jesus washed the feet of all His disciples. He was willing to be the

servant. We wash each others' feet because Jesus asked us to do it too. We show that we are willing to be servants too."

Daddy put his socks and shoes back on. He took the bowl of water to the table. Mommy and Daddy and Daniel prayed that Jesus would take away their sins.

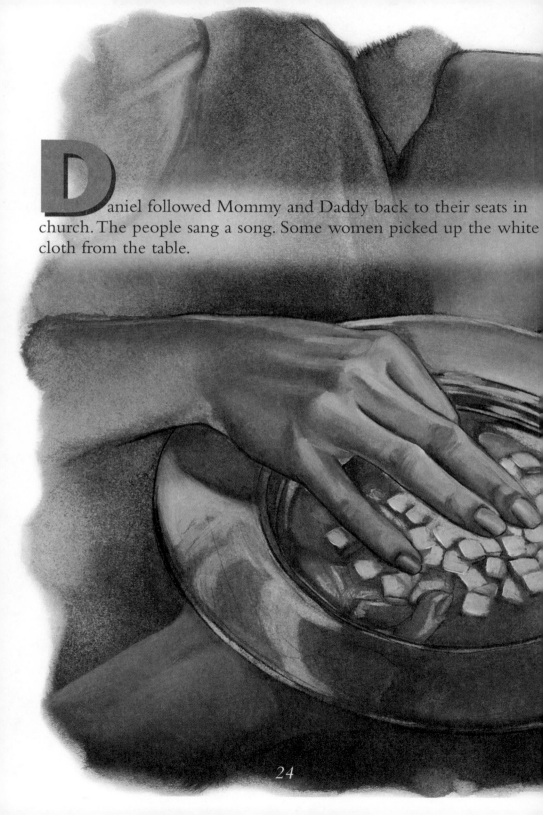

**D**aniel followed Mommy and Daddy back to their seats in church. The people sang a song. Some women picked up the white cloth from the table.

**D**aniel saw shiny plates on the table with pieces of flat bread on them. He saw large shiny trays with small glasses of grape juice.

Pastor David prayed. He thanked Jesus for the bread. Then he broke the bread into small pieces with his fingers. Some men picked up the plates. They let each person take one piece of the flat bread.

astor David read from his Bible. "Jesus wants us to eat the bread and remember Him," he said. And then all the people ate their little piece of bread.

The men picked up the trays of juice and gave each person a tiny glass.

Pastor David prayed. He thanked Jesus for the grape juice. He read his Bible again. "Jesus wants us to drink the juice and remember Him," he said. Everyone drank their little glass of juice.

Then the men picked up the little glasses. The women covered the table with the white cloth.

Pastor David stood up and spoke to the church. Then the people sang a song, and Pastor David prayed. He stretched his arms out over the people. He said, "Amen!" Church was over.

**A**t bedtime, Mommy asked, "Did you have a nice day?"
"Oh, yes," Daniel said. "What is my story about tonight?"

Daniel's story was about living in heaven with Jesus. Mommy told him that we will be very happy there. No one will cry or be sad. The animals and plants will not die, and the animals will be friendly.

We will live with all of God's people who have ever lived on the earth, even people we read about in the Bible! Best of all, we get to live with Jesus forever, because He died for our sins.

Mommy finished and said, "Now, let's pray."

**A**nd Daniel prayed this prayer.

"Dear God,

"Thank You that Jesus died for me to take away my sins. I'm sorry for the bad things I do. Please forgive me. I know that You will always love me no matter what. Thank You for Mommy and Daddy and the baby that we are going to have. Thank You for loving us. Please look after us all. In Jesus' name, amen."

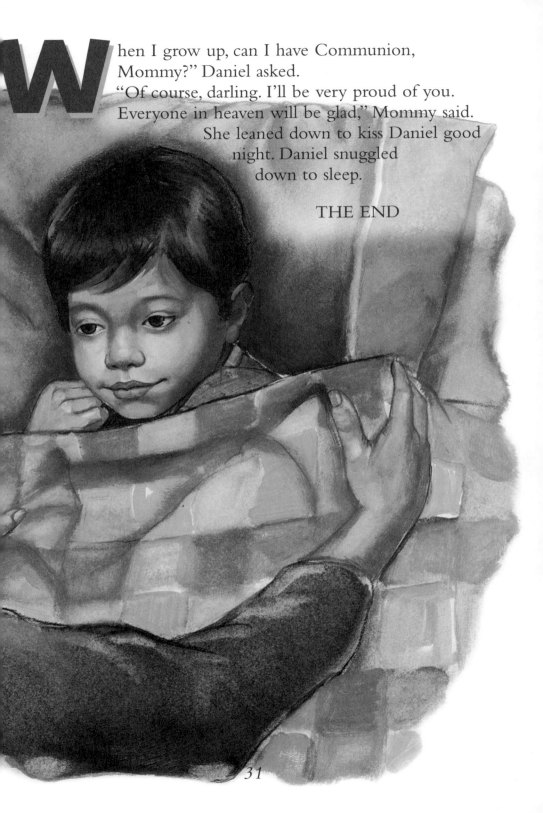

**W**hen I grow up, can I have Communion, Mommy?" Daniel asked.

"Of course, darling. I'll be very proud of you. Everyone in heaven will be glad," Mommy said.

She leaned down to kiss Daniel good night. Daniel snuggled down to sleep.

**THE END**

# For Parents

This book is designed to teach our precious children about two of the meaningful rites of passage in our church—baptism and Communion. For children, the practices may seem strange and inexplicable at times.

The stories were written for the real Daniel, my son, who is now eight years old. The baby in the stories that was not yet born at the time turned out to be his little brother, Michael. Writing these stories and sharing them with my sons has helped them to love Jesus even more and to appreciate what Jesus has done for them, because they are sons of God.

The boys loved having the stories read to them when they were smaller, and they now love to read them for themselves. I have had them illustrate the text during a long church service, and they have made very precious books and found creative ways to express their take on the services. I am always in awe of the understanding that children have for spiritual things.

Observation with appropriate explanation is a good way to introduce your child to the wonder of God's gifts to us of salvation and redemption. The topics can also be introduced by looking them up in the Bible. Here are some good texts: **Baptism**—Matthew 3:11–16; Mark 1:4–11; Luke 3:21, 22 and 7:29, 30; John 1:29–36; Acts 2:38–41 and 8:12 and 10:47, 48; 1 Corinthians 12:13. **Communion**—Matthew 26:17–30; Mark 14:12–26; Luke 22:1–20. There are some excellent videos and DVDs about Jesus that can gently introduce the topic of Jesus' mission and sacrifice. You can also find songs children can learn and coloring books for church or home, especially at Easter time.

The best time to read this book to your child is just before a baptism or Communion service, to familiarize them with the procedure and get them to match the pictures with the events they see on the day. This will keep them involved in the service. The child could also participate by bringing a flower, a bookmark, or a card they have made to give to the baptismal candidate, to welcome him or her into the church. We have found that explaining Communion to our sons helps to underline the solemnity of the occasion and instill the respect with which the Communion service should be approached.

May God bless you and your little ones as you teach them about the God who loves us more than we can ever fathom, and may we all meet in heaven one day soon.